Lessons With The Beloved

—————— A dialogue with God ——————

by

Mary Ann Hobson

iUniverse, Inc.
New York   Bloomington

Lessons With The Beloved

iUniverse books may be ordered through booksellers or by contacting:

*iUniverse
1663 Liberty Drive
Bloomington, IN 47403
www.iuniverse.com
1-800-Authors (1-800-288-4677)*

*ISBN: 978-1-4401-1557-8 (pbk)
ISBN: 978-1-4401-1556-1 (ebk)*

Printed in the United States of America

iUniverse rev. date: 1/05/09

Acknowledgment from Author

This book is a product of my Spirit's contact with the Other Side, the Spirit World, and their messages of love. With their wisdom I wrote the lessons that I was given. Without their wisdom this book could not have been written. I have tried to do my best in putting these lessons on paper in order to share them with all who choose to read them. And if this book is within your hands, maybe it is your Spirit's way of gently encouraging for you to start on your own Spiritual path and journey.

I have not changed the lessons and their order in how I received them. As I believe they were given in this order for a reason. I have put Father God's words in Italics to make it easier for the reader to distinguish our dialogue. I give my utmost gratitude and love to our Father God, to his Council and to my Spirit Guide, Manalan.

I also like to thank my dearest friends S. Wedde, R. Flowers, H.Dogan, J. Copeland, and R. Eidson. Friends are the priceless gifts we are given.

Mary Ann

****

Gently, I close my eyes.

My mind's eye awakens,

My body relaxes and

The physical earth fades away.

There I find old and new friends.

There I find Old and Young Spirits,

Who exist peacefully,

And their loving messages flow.

Like a gentle breeze in my mind.

Acknowledgements from Father God

"The words in this Book are to be taken for what they are worth but never to put my image in words, as they are just words. Your God exists within your hearts not in any words. Therefore, when you are reading this book please try not to dwell on the words as they are only a reflection of the Spirit of your God. You are to read to open your minds and Spirits to my being not to identify with any book. This book comes as a message to you but not within words that limit my presence, as your God. There are no words to describe my presence but you are to come to that conclusion yourselves. There will be times when you are seeking God in your books, but God is only found in your hearts and minds. Therefore, please seek God within yourselves."

To

My loving family,

Thank you for allowing me to keep

One foot in Heavens while helping me

Keep the other foot on Earth.

I love you.

Contents

Preface.. xv

Introduction... xxi

Lesson One – *Love For the Animals* 1

Lesson Two – *Love for Self and Others*............................6

Lesson Three – *How to Be Your Best Self*........................11

Lesson Four – *The Families You Chose*............................18

Lesson Five – *The Universe and You* 26

Lesson Six – *The Underworld*...31

Lesson Seven – *The Earth* 35

Lesson Eight – *The Council* 37

Lesson Nine – *My Children*...41

Lesson Ten – *The Harm* 46

Lesson Eleven – *Afterlife*...51

Lesson Twelve – *The Other Side*.......................................60

Conclusion from the Author 66

Conclusion from my Spirit Guide, Manalan 67

Conclusion from the Beloved 68

Preface

Many years ago when I came across to the book *Conversations with God*, written by Neale Donald Walsch, I remember wondering how it can be possible for a person to have conversations with God. Who in their right mind would even claim to have a conversation with God? With the Creator, who created the heaven and earth. I read these books in order to see and feel what this author was talking about. My heart never doubted the authors claim but my human mind had difficulty accepting such claim. Upon the completion of reading the first couple books, I was touched and humbled by the loving conversation within these books. I was glad to have come across to them and enjoyed reading them. It was obvious that the contents of these books were written with love and given to this author with love from God. At that time, I did not realize my own Spirit's thirst for seeking and finding answers to my own spiritual growth and existence.

We are all the children of our eternal Father God and Mother God. They have entrusted in giving our care to the hands of our earthly mothers and fathers whom we are born to on this side of our existence. What an honor it is to be able to have and be given the chance to raise and/or love a child of this world.

Children come through our human bodies, but they don't belong to us. We can teach them what we know, but they will also develop their own thoughts. We are the temporary mothers and fathers to old and young spirits that come and go following their own spiritual paths and life charts.

Most people grow up with an idea and a sense of God. Even though we don't see or talk with Father God, we believe in his Divine Spirit and in his Divine Plan. Your Spirit knows the existence of someone greater, no matter how you may define him, what you may call him, or how you worship. We are created from our Beloved Father's Spirit; therefore, we are all a part of his loving Spirit.

Beloved Father talks with many of his children. Conveying his love to us in many ways, but sometimes we neglect to see and acknowledge this wisdom and exchange. Our father does not selectively choose whom he speaks to; he speaks to those who seek and speak to him. He hears and sees the needs of all his children, and he is always attentive to all his children and those who need him the most, who are poor, sick, weak, hungry, and orphans around the world. Father God loves each one of his children unconditionally and he is always with us. He does not play favorites, and loves you no matter who you are, what color you are, how you look and whatever your beliefs may be.

One should attend religious services not to find God there, as he is always with us and everywhere. But, instead we should gather in our chosen religious congregations to worship and celebrate the presences of Beloved Father and Mother God. Religions were established in accordance with God's laws; in order to create peace and harmony among people, not to further divide ourselves from each other. If there is to be peace, we need to respect and tolerate each other and each other's beliefs. Peace is within us and when we are gentle, tolerant and respectful to each other we use this peace and encourage others to do the same.

When we raise our greater consciousness by opening our minds and spirits, we are capable of using our mind's eye to converse not only with the spirit world, but also with our Beloved Father. I did not seek him or call upon him, he came when the time was right. We, as the children of this world come in different colors and sizes. We are born in faraway places from each other, speaking in different languages. However, we have more in common than what we see as our differences. We come from the same source, the great loving spirit of our Father God. The Beloved Father is the creator of this world and the witness to our actions. He has never been absent from his position, and he continues to manage our Universe and all its inhabitants.

We should never fear God the Father, for he loves all of us and he would not approve any person on his behalf to create fear within us about his presence and being. He is merciful, compassionate, gentle, caring, and loving to all of his children equally. We were not created in perfection and for this reason we are given the choice of living in the lives we select in order to become greater spirits. We accomplish this by living a loving and a peaceful life. We are to strive to learn more by helping others, ourselves and by expanding our minds.

Father God is the only one who can present himself to you, and he does this in many ways. However, he has given all of us the same gifts, out of his love and protection. Our bodies, physically and spiritually are created like a master piece. Our physical body parts and organs have special purposes, working together like the inside mechanics of a clock, so we can continue to exist. There is also a greater plan of design for what our eyes cannot see within our physical bodies, like our spirit, soul and mind. I like to believe that the most important gift is our Spirit. Although we may not be aware of it, it is awake, alert and amazing. It has been with us for a long time, for many life times, and it will be with us to eternity. Beloved Father does not ask much in return. Our well being, learning to better ourselves continuously and helping each other and for being the best person we can be.

As for myself, I learn more each day from the spirits on the other side, not only about them but of my own self too. I value and respect my relationship with my Spirit Guide, Manalan. I am appreciative of his wisdom, guidance, and the time he shares with me. However, I learn most from my daily life on this earth, where I meet and interact with wonderful people and experience new and different events. I also encounter hardships of life, but I am able to make more sense out of them while realizing there is a greater purpose for everything.

Keep your hearts and minds open to all who surround you, as we all have much to learn from each other and about each other. We are all here together, at this time, at this place, and for a reason. Let's not be afraid to open our hearts, minds, and spirits to each other and to the other side as well. Our physical bodies will become old and/or sick, and we will once again make our journey back home. We will then realize how much further we have learned and accomplished. On the Other Side, we will once again become whole and healthy and be greeted by our loved ones, teachers, guides, and the Beloved Father and Mother.

Introduction

We all have inner thoughts. It is that voice we sometimes hear and accept as our own mind thinking aloud. Some of these thoughts are created by our own mind and sometimes they may be from a greater source. They may be subtle hints or messages from the Angels, Spirit Guides and even from the Divine Beloved Father and Mother. Those people who have been on their own spiritual search or have awakened may be more aware as to the origins of their own thoughts. Regardless, we all need to be more aware of our own thoughts and respect them by respecting our own selves in mind, body, and spirit.

These thoughts from the Other Side flow with positive elements and with loving but helpful messages. In the midst of our busy lives, many people are not aware of their own thoughts as they continue with their daily tasks. For this reason they are unable to distinguish between their own thoughts and the gentle messages of the Spirit world. In order for our Spirits to elevate, we need to raise our consciousness by paying special attention to what we are doing, what we are saying, what we are feeling and how we are impacting the lives of others and our Universe. By being thoughtful and showing kindness to others, we open doors for greater spiritual learning and wisdom. We should continuously strive to think better, be gentler, help others and live as peaceful as we can. We were created from the love of our Beloved Father and only with love all things are possible.

Many months ago I was awakened to my clairaudience, which I would describe as being able to open my mind to thoughts coming to my mind from the Other Side, the Spirit World. It is not always easy to understand and make sense out of these thoughts. I am still in the process of learning, as there is much to learn and awaken to. Just as there are many people who have great gifts of writing and playing beautiful music, painting beautiful pictures, having the ability to write great stories, the spirit is also capable of receiving and having gifts. There are many people who are clairaudient and there are many more people with other great gifts and fascinating skills. These people and their gifts bring peaceful conversations and make us aware that life continues after death.

I believe in my heart, that one day all people will be awakened in mind and spirit and will communicate directly with the Spirits on the other side. And it will be normal; people will not be shunned, persecuted, classified as crazy, doubted or politely told what a great imagination they have.

In 1800's, I am certain many people would have doubted that we would be able to put a tool to our ear and hear the voice of another person. But, today the telephone is an everyday item, and not a big deal. We have been so busy looking and improving our physical lives that we have neglected to develop and become familiar with our own spirit. As our Spirits reincarnate and become more evolved over centuries, we are adjusting and awakening to greater levels of spiritual functioning.

What we call psychics, are those people who have allowed their spirits to reach beyond the tools we are all given, our basic senses. Genuine Psychics come from a loving world of white light and enlightenment. They offer loving messages of continuity of life after death. Of course, there is good and bad in all people, and there will be people who claim to be Psychics and take advantage of the weak and create fear. Sadly, there are many people in the world whose aim is purely to make money; this form of greed exists among all professions, not just among Psychics. As I like to say, "You come with nothing and you go with nothing, so what you do in between is your own decision". I cannot tell you who is genuine and not, however, please seek that answer from within your own self, as you probably know it. Also, please keep in mind that psychics are also human and they also make mistakes. I like to think that if we knew everything, we would not be here. A person should not depend on the skills of a psychic; instead they should strengthen their own spiritual selves. Instead of paying a Psychic, give that money to someone who is hungry, sick or old and say a little prayer. This will make you feel as good as any Psychic would and in return you may be in the prayers of that person whom you helped.

Our Spirits are great and complex, they are the greatest gift we have all been given. At present, our Spirit is in Human Form. However, there happens to be many spirits who are not in Human form at this time. These are the spirits whom I and many others communicate with. They were also in human form and lived as great people on this Earth many times, just like you and I are currently. Their communication and messages are almost always loving, caring, positive and appreciative.

A Spirit Guide is a spirit who comes with you, to guide you on this Earth. They were with us before we were born and gently guide you as you live in your current life. Most people are not aware of their Spirit Guide, and you don't really need to. However, you can talk to them, and know in your hearts that they hear you. There are times when Guides are able to communicate with their persons whom they are guiding. My Spirit Guide, Manalan is a communicating Spirit Guide and I feel blessed for his presence. He guides, helps, and teaches me with love and patience.

After my awakening to being clairaudient, I was humbled with the opportunity to speak with Father God on couple occasions only. When I meditate, I usually speak with my Spirit Guide and/or other Spirits on the other side. One day, Manalan told me that I would have twelve messengers. I wasn't sure what he was talking about. I thought possibly that I would meet twelve Spirit Messengers or twelve people who had some kind of something for me. And I put that conversation and subject aside. Until one day, when Manalan communicated that Father God wanted to talk to me and then he stepped aside. Father God stated that he would like to talk to me about certain topics, and I was to write these down.

The next day during my meditation, I had my tape recorder prepared, I closed my eyes and he spoke. It was much easier to understand him as he came more clearly to my mind than other spirits, including my guide Manalan. Father God chose the first eleven lessons, including their titles and content. The twelfth lesson, The Other Side was my request as I was very curious about the Other Side. After these twelve lessons, my conversation of two weeks ago with my Guide came to my memory and I knew that I had misunderstood the twelve messengers, it was twelve messages. Father God's lessons were always very timely and the same amount of time in length. I was always impressed by Father God's time keeping. He knew when to start, when to stop, and always seemed to take the same amount of time for each lesson. He conveyed his concerns and messages. Some lessons were in more detail. For example, Father God spoke more about the earth however, I was not always able to understand through my knowing and be able to put on paper later. I did try to do my best to present what was given to me.

During my initial conversation with our Beloved Father, I had asked him what he would want people to know about him. He had stated "tell people not to fear God, because I love them". The gentleness of his message was very touching and I will always remember that first conversation we had. I don't know what I was expecting to hear, but this had truly touched me.

This book is about the lessons and knowledge that I had personally received from the Beloved Father. I hand wrote and transferred the given lessons from my tape recorder to my traditional note pad, and then I typed my notes on the computer. When I finished, I felt relieved as if weight was taken off my shoulders. Although I was not asked or required to meet everyday for a lesson with Father, somehow I felt personally responsible to do so and enjoyed them also. After the lessons were completed, I tried to find a book agent. As you may already suspect, I did not find one. Actually, I found many but they did not find the book or writer suitable for publishing. Although disappointed, I understood them and could not blame them. This is when I decided to publish this book myself as my own Birthday and Christmas gift to myself. Lessons with the Beloved were the best gift I have received and I feel blessed to be able to share it.

There are numerous people who speak with Father God and other Spirits. Each and every person seems to have their own reality, sources and knowledge. I don't find myself in the position to judge or evaluate another person's experiences. I cannot explain why my information I receive is different from the information that another medium/person may receive from the Spirit World. I wish I did have a magic answer, but I don't. Personally, these matters do not bother me; however, I am sure it is in the minds of many others. There are many things that I cannot explain and know the answer to, but I try to do my best and come from a place of peace, love, and white light. I see myself as a tool for God, not God. In Lessons with the Beloved, I tried to represent Father God's thoughts and wishes as clear as I understood them, with his gentleness and care.

There are many names given to describe God in all religions and cultures. Within my writings, I interchangeably use the names Beloved, Beloved Father, Father (God), Father God, and God. At the end of the road, we are all talking about the same Divine Source whom we are a part of, whom we love, whom we pray to, whom we talk with, and whom we feel his Divine presence.

I hope and wish that reading this book, will create a thirst within you to search and explore your own spirituality. And as you find your own spiritual answers and paths, your spirit will find a place of peace, comfort and joy. This is my experience, these were the lessons given to me and I wish that it will reach the hands of many people. After you have read this book please don't put it away, give it to someone else. I realize that sometimes there is a greater reason for our actions and the things we must do in order to be of service to the world we live in and all its' inhabitants. Writing and publishing this simple and short book is one of those actions on my behalf.

And this is our story and my lessons. Thank you for reading them.

Blessed be.

Mary Ann Hobson

******

Lesson One – Love For the Animals

"The animals were given to you from our love here. Tell them that animals are there for the love of God and when people show their love to animals, they show their love to me also. I created the animals after I created people. People were lonely and they needed a spirit that can be their friend forever in the heavens and on earth. There are different kinds of animals. They were created so you can enjoy their presence and being. Some of them came with a purpose and some came only to be with you."

"Father, can you give some examples of the animals that have a greater purpose?"

"Yes. The cow provides you meat and milk. The cow provides you sustenance for living."

"Father, how did you create the cow?"

"I created the cow from the branches of trees and then I breathed life in them and they moved. The cow is significant because this is the mother of all animals, for it gives you food. You have to treat cow with gentleness and respect because he gives you life and you need to take well care of them."

"I have heard that in India people treat cow as sacred Father. Why?"

"Yes, they made a particular cow sacred because he was very brave and he was not going to be slaughtered by people. Because he showed a great spirit he was respected by these people in India. The cow will be with you forever, as long as you care well for them."

"What is another animal with a greater purpose?"

"The horse also has a greater purpose, but not like the cow. The horse was brought in order to help people who needed a way to get places far and away from their homes."

"Father, how did you create the horse?"

"I looked at the heavens and I found objects that has the spirit of a large thunder. Then I took the rocks from under my feet, because, he had to be heavy. Then I placed my love and blended them and they formed the body of this animal. And when I blew my spirit into this form, he ran like thunder under my feet. People need to ride them in order to love them. They will fall in love with the spirit of the horse, because his spirit is magnificent like the thunder that you fear".

"Father, what is another animal with a greater purpose?"

"There is the Elephant. I made him from the Seas. He was a very large animal, and he occupied a vast body. He was slightly senseless, so I put a very gentle spirit in him and he came to help you pull heavy things on earth. When he walked, his feet shook the earth he walked on. He was powerful but also very weak; he was to obey people who

needed him. The Elephant is the sound of your earth and they need to be loved and cared for by people."

"What is another animal with a greater purpose?"

"This is the Camel. I created the Camel as a companion to people who lived in the dessert. The camel has a great form and they can tolerate the heat and the sun. I made him from the horse but supplied much more so he can handle the world's desserts. The Camel was an ordinary horse, but I blew a bubble on his back so he can store water in it. People need to be very careful with the camel because I gave the Camel a great intellect. They have great memory and they will remember all things. They were given a mind that will remember the roads they travel on in the dessert but they will turn on you if you mistreat them, they will bite and harm you."

"What is another animal with a greater purpose?"

"Yes, there was the Tiger. He was a mighty spirit. I created him from the bones of all the other animals; therefore, he had many qualities within him. He is brave, he is mighty but you are to fear him because he is the protector of the Universe. And he is easily upset by all around him. They need to take great protection when dealing with the Tiger. He is not a companion animal and he will harm you in order to save his own self. Unlike the other animals, the Tiger will not protect or serve you."

"Father, what is another animal with a greater purpose?"

"*There is the Lion. He is the Master of the Gardens. He is the mother of all around him. He is the life force that is capable of giving and taking from you. I wanted a great spirit who would protect the territories of the other animals and he was the one who would do this. He will strike you when you least expect it and devour you in minutes.*"

"Is there another animal with greater purpose?"

"*There is the donkey. He is not very smart but he is tough and his body can handle many things that others can't. The donkey can yell very loud and he will hear his own path. He can travel a long distance because his lungs are large. His legs are short but strong. I made the donkey from a small horse that had no purpose. So, I changed his physical body and gave him strength to carry heavy things. The donkey needs respect and allow him to be stubborn because he is very set in his own ways. He will do what he wants to do and you need to respect this animal for his stubbornness.*"

"Father, what about the Snake?"

"*He doesn't have a greater purpose. I made the snake to crawl, so he can sweep the floor under your feet. He was a great animal but he had lessons to learn and he was not willing to learn. So, I made him crawl close to the earth, so he will always hear the vibrations of the earth and learn from it. You should be aware of him because he is dangerous to you. His venom is mighty poisonous because this is his only protection. He is to protect himself from others but the others will not respect him.*"

****

"*When you learn to love and respect the spirits of the animals than you can also learn to respect your own spirit. You must master the love of animals because they are there to teach your spirit lessons. They are not below you. You are below them because they don't live in fear like you. They live to enjoy life and to help you through your life. Teach your children to love and respect the animals that were created for you and to help you. By loving them you also love me.*"

Lesson Two – Love for Self and Others

"When I created the world I promised that people would be intelligent and superior to others. In the hierarchy of all living things. There are times when people are not using their intelligence in order to serve our needs here. But there are many times when people do serve us in order to better their lives."

"Yes, I hear you father."

"Your mission is to convey to my people that I am with them at all times and I will always give them the strength to be better than what they are and whom they choose to be. I created the world within seven days of the week but you have managed to make it more than what it is. The people of our earth need to awaken their spirits more in order to have more peace and harmony among themselves. When I created the universe I made sure that all of my beings would have plenty of everything. And they would think and survive through many disasters to come to your lives. The Universe contains all things possible because I made it so there is enough for all. I know that there are people who are very sick and starving in my world but this is not because of me, it is because of the leaders whom arise amongst them. They learned to

make people's lives miserable by controlling the amounts of food supply and other needed elements. These people who are harming my children all over the world will answer to themselves when their path leads them here. Then they will remember the things they did and will have a chance to be better people in the afterlife."

"Yes Father, I understand."

"My children, all of my children are of my spirit and they are a part of my existence. When people are unnecessarily hurting each other by means of violence or starvation, they are also hurting me in return. I am a powerful being but I also feel the pain and misery of my people there. I never meant to have so many of my children being harmed by each other. There will come a time when we will all be reunited and then I will ask those people what their purpose was on earth. They will than look back and remember the promises they made when they left here and descended to earth."

"Father, does every spirit make a plan to achieve certain things before they come to earth?"

"Yes. You and every single one of you made plans to live a certain life in order to achieve certain things. Many people do live great lives, stay on a positive path, and achieve good things. But there are people who forget their desires when they come to earth and follow the path of another creator than me."

"What other creator are you talking about?"

"There is a darker spirit that encourages people to do terrible things that I would not tolerate and some of you

follow this path with him and it leads you to his existence. Not to mine."

"Father, what are the examples of things that people do that leads them to the darker existence?"

"Yes, when they kill another human being, I am no longer with them. They have killed a child of mine and I don't forgive this. This is my one exception to my leaving your spirit alone."

"Is this painful to you?"

"Yes, of course it is. I love all my beings and when I have to let one go, it makes me sad also. But I realize that this is the only thing I can do for them. There will be times when you will feel alone and during those times you must remember that I am always with you. I love you very much."

"What happens to that spirit after he is with the darker existence?"

"You don't need to be wondering about that. You don't need to entertain thoughts about the darker existence. It is a waste of your intelligence and spirit that is white and pure."

"Thank you Father."

"There will be times when you will suffer great deal of pain and once again you must remember that I am with you always. There will be times when you will be confronted with evil things and you must remember that I am always with you. There will be times when you will think of doing or saying things that are harmful to each other and during

those times you will need to learn to be gentle and loving to each other."

"Yes Father."

"Remember that your bodies were created out of my mind but your spirit came from within me and I made it all possible with my love and compassion. When you learn to love your own self, you learn to love me. And when you love others like I do, than you love me."

"Father, why is it so hard for some people to love others?"

"They have chosen to not love any longer. They need to be reminded of my greater love within them."

"How can a person remind themselves to love?'

"You don't have to look very far my dear. You need to just open your eyes and spirit to others and the love shall overflow into you. And there will be people who are to test your love on earth."

"What do you mean?"

"What I meant is that I have many children and when you do something good for each other, I am aware of this love interaction. And I make sure that all my love flows through you."

"I see."

"Love is the greatest emotion I have given to all my children. There will be times when love seems so far away

from your hearts but remember that it is a near as you make it possible. Love is created by you and no one else but you. Your love shines through your bodies when you feel it and when you love others, you share this great light with them. Peace and Love will bring you home to me and I will always love you. No matter where you are or what you are doing. Love one another, respect one another and feel my greater love all around yourselves. I loved you so much that I created the heaven and earth for you. Now please love what I created and take care of it just as I would."

"Thank you Father."

****

"Love is like a stream of water, it runs through you in your blood. It runs under you and it runs over you. Love yourself and you will love me."

Lesson Three – How to Be Your Best Self

"This is very important to me because the better you are to yourself, the better you will be in all aspects of your life. Prior to your spirit coming here, you are given certain qualities which enable you to function at a greater level."

"What are those qualities?"

"I am talking about your sense of being. Your spirit comes in several layers and each one of these layers enables you to emit energies directed at your own self and to the Universe around you."

"Is there a part of our spirit that is in touch with the other side?"

"Yes, there is a layer of your spirit that we control directly from here. This is the esoteric layer. It is where your sense of function is at and this is the layer that we instruct in order for you to lead a life that is prosperous and content. Your esoteric layer also has many levels. There are seven levels."

"What are those levels?"

"The first level is your intuition, where your psychic skills are stored. The second level is your guidance. This is how we approach you and how we can be in contact with you."

"How are we contacted by the spirit world?"

"We can play with the energies around you, so you will know of our existence around you. Your spirit hears many sounds and vibrations and we are able to tap into this level of your spirit."

"I see"

"The third level is what you send out from your own body. Your body emits energies and when you are using this level; your spirit is heard by the Universe and us. When you are praying and talking to us you are using this level. The Fourth Level is where all your memories of past lives are stored. You can't tap into this level as you will not need to use this level, unless if you are having difficulty from a prior life. There are people who tap into this level of your Spirit while conducting Hypnosis. This is also where your Karmic energy is stored and this is where it stays for you."

"Father, why do people experience difficulties from their past lives?"

"When you reincarnate your body is programmed so it has no memory of its past lives. Some spirits don't want to let go of their past lives and when they reincarnate they experience difficulties from stemming from their past lives. It can be disturbing to their current life and they can seek the help of individuals who can assist them."

"What can a person do if they feel disturbed by a past life memory?"

"If you believe you are having residual memories from the past, you must have your spirit awakened to current state. This is possible to be done by your people who conduct Hypnosis. You must be willing to let go of the past memory and ask for guidance from us. When you seek us, we will know and we will respond to you."

"I see"

"The Fifth level to your Spirit is your awakened layer. This is where your new learning is stored and you continue to grow in order to learn more. Your Spirit will remember all of what it has learned. You are not aware of this level because your senses don't feel its existence."

"Will we remember everything?"

"Yes, you will but some of your memories will be more prominent than others, depending on its importance for your own growth and choice."

"I can understand that, as I seem to remember some things more clearly than others in my current life."

"The Sixth level is a harder part of your spirit. It protects you from the outside energies and it also gives you guidance. Your Spirit Guides come to your Sixth level because they are capable of accessing this layer with you."

"Does every person have a Spirit Guide?"

"Yes, all my children come with a guide to ease the pain of your transition and life in general. They will guide you and protect you always."

"Why don't we all have an awareness of our Spirit Guides?"

"Many people don't have an awareness of their guides because there is no need to be aware of their work. Their work is to help you and to protect you by giving you inner voices that will be heard by your Spirit only."

"Can people communicate directly with their Spirit Guides?"

"Yes, they can and they have this ability if it is developed. However, people are not given this ability because they would depend too much on their guides and use less of their own minds and spirits to learn from. People can develop this ability, but it is not easy to be in tune with your own self."

"How do some people know and communicate with their Spirit Guides?"

"A person can choose to go into a greater level of their spirit and become more awakened and be able to communicate with their Spirit Guides. For example, you had a great desire and you were able to tap into this level of your Spirit."

"Yes. I understand."

"The Seventh Level of your Spirit is the larger level. This level emits energies and colors into your existence."

"What do you mean?"

"Your body has Auras. Which are energies that are produced by your Spirit and these energies have colors of the Rainbow to shine for you. Your body uses them when you are experiencing pain, happiness and other emotion that are felt. When we see an Aura transmitting certain colors, we can easily identify and be aware of your presence and attend to you."

"What do you mean by attend to us?"

"We look after you. We have special ways of caring for one's body and mind. We can achieve this by emanating energies from our side to your Aura, so it can be in a greater presence then it is. We come to you when you are ill and your Auras are the signal signs that alert our attention."

"The Human Body and Spirit are truly amazing Father."

"Yes it is. It is very complicated but it serves a greater need than what you can see and feel with your senses."

"Father, how do we be our best self?"

"You are to achieve many things. Your body, mind and spirit will automatically guide you, as it was designed to do this. You are to know this and learn to listen to your own self. When you are doing something that is good, you feel good and when you are doing something that is bad, you don't feel good. When you are feeling good, your mind, body and spirit will also feel good. When you don't feel good; your Mind, Body and Spirit also suffer. You are to be a good person, show kindness to your people and utilize what is given to you by me."

"Are we all here to achieve many and great things?"

"Everyone comes with a different reason and sometimes it is not always to achieve a lot but to serve a purpose for others."

"What do you mean by to serve a purpose for others?"

"People must have a contrast. A variety of people come to life with you, otherwise you would have nothing and no one to learn from."

"How about the poor, did they want to be poor?"

"They have chosen this life because they wanted a difficult life in order to learn the most. You are to be generous and kind to my children who have chosen a difficult life to live in. I am amongst them and I see their struggles. I watch them and see all things possible for them but they don't always see their own possibilities."

"How about the handicapped, did they also choose their lives?"

"Yes, they have also chosen their own lives. Some spirits come this way and some come normal and later they become handicapped so they can compare their experiences of both worlds."

"I see."

******

"*You are to appreciate all you have and stop thinking as if you are the center of this Universe, because you are not. There are important things to do and achieve. Each one of you must know your purpose and seek higher knowledge when necessary. We are here to guide you but your desires must be sincere and then it is our responsibility to help and guide you. Take care of yourselves and of each other. Remember, when you care for others, you also care for me.*"

Lesson Four – The Families You Chose

"Your lives were chosen by yourselves. But, we also have an input as to locations that you come to when you decide to enter this side of your existence. You have chosen the very family you came into, because they matched the lessons you were to learn from. Their lessons that they can offer you is what we seek for within their homes. For this reason you chose your own Family and Homes."

"Yes."

"There are many different types of people on this earth and they all offer something to learn from. Their journeys have taken them through many different roads and they have obtained what they know and received from their experiences. When a Spirit chooses a family to come to, it is a very deliberate act on that spirit's behalf. You chose the right mother, the right father and the right family system that would best serve your needs. The places you choose to come are the elements for your growth and learning. We guide you so that it is a sound decision for you and then you are left alone."

"What do you mean?"

"*I mean that you are to live and to learn alone for your own spiritual growth. You are to be as bright as you can in order to learn the most you can from the life you have chosen.*"

"Do we know our past and present families whom we choose?"

"*Your Ancestors were of many because they also lived many lives as you have. Therefore, no one can really say where you are from or what you have experienced. Your bloodlines may be of one origin but your spirits are of another origin. There are many twists and turns in your lives so you can grow and learn more. There will be times when the lives you have chosen are very difficult and you will come into the midst of turmoil.*"

"What do you mean by turmoil?"

"*I mean that you may come into unfavorable conditions that may delay your learning and growth. But regardless, you can overcome these if you put your best self forward.*"

"I see,"

"*Your Mothers and Fathers take on the roles of us here. They raise you in order for you to flourish and be independent. But they can't live your life for you, as you must explore and discover your own strengths. You came into the families you have chosen according to the level of your spirit. It is your decision what you will do when you come to live on earth and within the lives you have chosen. There will be plenty of opportunities for you to acknowledge and seek to learn from.*"

"What do you mean by opportunities?"

"*There will be many chances of developing and improving your spirit's direction. This is up to your own desires. There are times when people's desires are lacking and they don't seek higher learning. However, there are also many people with high desires who make the most of their chosen lives.*"

"Yes,"

"*Your aim and desire to be perfect is not to be wondered about. I have personally given each and every one of you the desire to excel in all things to come to you. But it is up to your own selves to utilize these given skills. There will be times when life will be challenging and frustrating, but you must never lose the sight of the things you want to gain and learn from. I gave you a life span that is long enough to learn the lessons you came to live and seek.*"

"Yes,"

"*Many times I hear people asking, "why did I come into this family?" and my response to you is, "you chose them yourself." Then they say "but I would have never chosen this family." Then I remind them that it was their free will that made this decision, not I. I made it so you have free will and to take advantages of all things offered to you. There will be times when you don't do this, but this is also a part of the Master Plan of all things. I like to think that the lives you have chosen are the best for you. After all, you are to learn more than I, and I am to lead you to your destination.*"

"Do you hear the prayers that ask you for help?"

"Yes. There are times when I feel tempted to come and rescue you but I know that this is not the right thing to do for you. I made my decisions and you are to live your own desires. When you pray for help I hear your prayers. I will look after all my children and to a certain level I will attend to their needs."

"Thank you,"

"Your favorite Mothers and Fathers are usually from the most difficult lives you chose to come to. Although those were the most challenging lives you had, you grew the most intellectually and spiritually. I would never place any of my children knowingly into the harm's way, but you have free will and you selected your own homes that you came to."

"Father, there are children who are born in War torn countries where it continues to be dangerous. Did they also choose to go to these areas?"

"Yes. They chose this because it is dangerous and it is that danger they are seeking to learn and to grow from."

"How can a person grow from living in danger?"

"You can and you will. Your Spirit will enable you to grow in many ways. When children are born in countries where there is fighting going on, they grow up very quickly and they live each day of their life with intention. They may be in harm's way but they know better than this, because they know that their Spirit shall never die there."

"Father, there are children who are born in countries where there is severe poverty and hunger. Did they also choose to be there?"

"*These children are so brave. They come into countries where life is so difficult for them. They have a hard time finding food but they persist and become survivors among their own selves. They may seek food in the wilderness but their minds are never hungry. Their survival may be different from that of yours, but you must never forget that they are Spirits just like you. They deserve to be recognized and respected for the lives they have chosen.*"

"Yes, I feel that way also."

"*Their lives are as important as yours, if not even more important, because they experience so much tragedy and sadness that they evolve further and know more than you ever will know. You are to find compassion in your hearts in order to be better people and not forget the many people who are suffering in difficult lives. They could have chosen lives as easy as yours, but they chose a higher path in order to learn and grow more. You may have more things but they have more than you always.*"

"I understand."

"*Their eyes are not hungry like yours are. Their stomachs are hungry but their minds are full. Their lives are not wasted, they live forever like you do but they learn more when they exist among the harsh winds that are blowing around them. They have less but they have more.*"

"Yes, I witnessed this during my travels to those places where people were poor, but they had such richness to their spirits."

"Their mothers and fathers love them just like yours do but the only thing that they don't have is the financial help that you have. They love each other more than you do, because they have more time for each other. They are together and that is all that is important for them. All else will come and go but those spirits that are together will always stay close to each other. They give more time to simple things in life and you are too busy working for meaningless things that you already have plenty of. And in return, your spirits are lacking due to all your possessions."

"I understand. Do Spirits come together in order to be with each other?"

"Yes, they do. They come together to same places around same times. They like each other so much that they want to live together again."

"Is this a choice for all of us?"

"Yes. This is your choice but many of you cannot choose this way of living because you never developed your sense of family and well being."

"Father, what is your best advice in regards to family?"

"Appreciate who you are and the family you have come into. They may not be of the greatest people and greatest spirits but they made a home for you. You are to be appreciative of their efforts and what they have done for you. The lives of your families may be hard, but yours don't have to be unless if you choose to have it like this."

"If a person comes into a family where they are harmed by them, is it acceptable for this person to leave this family?"

"Yes, of course it is. There is nothing that you should tolerate that would harm you or your spirit. There are people in your countries who are equipped to handle such predicaments. But you must learn that it is about prevention not interruption of lives. There will be times when it is justly to remove a child from a home that is harmful. However, many times children are removed from homes that they are fine in and this is also wrong."

"Yes, it should be about prevention not interruption."

"The families you are with are temporary, but you have your entire lives to work on by yourselves and make the most of what is given to you. You should not judge your family for your own deficiency and weakness, as you are the creator of your own lives."

"When we come to the other side, will we be able to remember our families from our past lives?"

"Yes, you will have a sense of them but you will have no close emotional ties to them. Because, there will be hundreds of family members that you may have had from prior lives also. It is also your choice to acknowledge them."

"We have spoken a great deal on the family, what would you like to say to conclude this lesson in our minds Father?"

******

"Your Families are given to you upon your own choosing. And you need to make the most of them and their ways of being. You may have to live with them but you don't have to be like them. They also don't have to be like you. Their homes are a safe place for your Spirits. Families need to care well for each and every child that comes into their homes. You must remember that life is not always fair, but it is fair when it is your own choosing that deals your own faith."

Lesson Five – The Universe and You

"There are several things you should know about the Universe and your being. You are to open your mind and help people open their minds as to other living forms around the Universe. This is not to frighten people; it is just to teach them that they are not the only outer existence in the Outer Universe. There are many inhabitants besides you but they pose no threat to you. Their existence solely due to their makers and they are not harmful to your being."

"Father, why do we need to know about them?"

"As there may come a day, they may also evolve into greater beings. For this reason your people must strive harder in order to be more cognizant about the Universe and discover ways of protecting your being and preventing conflict, if there is to be Peace."

"Are we getting guidance and help from your side Father?"

"Yes, of course. We are constantly working here in order to help our people on earth. We also have master teachers and great spirits who are working on your behalf to help our people there."

"What can the ordinary person and people in general can do?"

"There are many things you must do in order to be more sensible and to protect your Universe. You need to keep it in good shape and care for it well so it doesn't ruin itself."

"What should we be doing to care better for the earth?"

"Look around you and you will see what I mean. You need to tell my people that their Universe is their home and they need to care for their home in order for them to live great lives and to secure a place for their own, the future of the human race."

"Father, there are many planets in the Universe. Is there life on these planets?"

"Yes, of course there is. There are many Planets in our Universe; we chose to live on earth because this dimension is very favorable to your bodies and existence. There is life on other planets also but they are from different species. Their leaders know us; we have mutual contracts and respect for each other's existence."

"Do you meet with them?"

"Yes, we meet regularly but we are not the closest friends as you may imagine. They are much more different than us."

"In what ways are they different from us?"

"*They have different values, morals and ethics than we do. Their lives are simpler; they live to be alive only. Not to work and seek greater things like you.*"

"Are they a danger to us?"

"*No, at present they pose no danger to our being. However, you should be aware that they do exist in order not to be afraid of them.*"

"What planet is there life at Father?"

"*There are several Planets where they exist, but the main planet they live in is Mars. Because this Planet can adjust its temperatures so it can accommodate life form of its own.*"

"Are they similar to us? Do they look like us?"

"*No, their bodies are composed of different materials than yours and they are not like you, because they don't have a Spirit like yours. Their bodies are made of strange materials that are not available in your world.*"

"Father, this brings me back to our being."

"*Yes. There are three realms to your dimension. What you see is not always what it is. You must wonder to your own self and become greater to seek and to find your own self.*"

"What do you mean?"

"*There are three components to your being.*"

"What are those?"

"The first area or level is where we keep our energy force that we supply you with as you descend on earth."

"What do you mean by energy force?"

"This is an energy force that feeds your body and mind. This is applicable to your spirit and you use this energy in order to think and be. This is given to all my children upon them leaving this side of our existence."

"I see"

"The next area or level is where we keep things that are needed in order for you to be a successful person. You are to pay special attention to this level because there are many tools available to you from this level. This is where you get your spiritual advice and needs met from."

"What do you mean?"

"This is the level and area you seek when you need comfort and health."

"I am confused about this level Father!"

"This is a level that is introduced to you as you live out your lives. But many people don't utilize this level because they don't ascend this high to seek it. For example, you have chosen to seek this level, because you are in contact with us and our energy. You chose this prior to going there but it is available to all as you live there."

"I see"

"There is a third level to your being and this is where we keep our own secrets."

"What do you mean by that?"

"This level is not accessible to you because you don't have a reason to seek anything from this dimension. There are many mystical reasons for us to have a place where we can keep our own divine secrets, because these are the elements we all need in order to survive and to prosper."

"I can respectfully understand that."

****

"Most people choose to live in a simple realm, with their earthly senses only. There is much more to your bodily functions than what you are using and given. It is more convenient and simple for people to focus on those things outside of their own being than to reflect and see what is within. For this reason most people don't seek further and choose only to use what they have all received. And, this is also fine."

Lesson Six – The Underworld

"Just as there is a higher level than your level of existence, there are levels to the Underworld. The Underworld is a level under your own level of existence and there are spirits there also, but they are different from yours. There are small and large creatures who all serve a greater purpose to your being and to our Earth. Their existence is not to please me but to serve me and what we need of them. They live many levels below you and they work very hard in order to bring beauty and peace to your lives."

"Why should we know about the Underworld?"

"Because, this is also of importance to your knowledge and you are to be aware of this level of creation. There are many levels to the Underworld and you must be open minded and seek to learn about them. These beings who are not visible to you serve great purposes. They help you in many ways, but their most important task is to be of service to your Earth. There are levels of classifications for our beings in the Underworld and they are in different levels of existence."

"Can you tell me about these levels?"

"Without going into greater detail about them, you should know about the levels that are closest to and the most important for you."

"What is that?"

"This level hosts numerous small creatures. You know them as Elves and Gnomes. They help the Earth by being brilliant and they complete many needed tasks for your Earth and in return for your existence."

"Like what?"

"What are the different tasks of the Elves and the Gnomes?"

"They cultivate the grounds of your earth and they fertilize the soils of your world as the soil also needs our assistance in order to be more productive. They work brilliantly with their minds. Elves were created to help us. Their short statures are very useful because they achieve many things with their small bodies. They help you by helping the earth under your feet. The Gnomes are the travelers who communicate with us here. They come here when they have a need and they seek our advice and return to the Underworld. They are all very mystical creatures with sharp minds and they are capable of achieving many things. They work hard and they help us in many ways."

"As mystical as they may be, it sounds very magical to us here."

"Yes, I know. They do exist and their presences have been expressed to you in your stories and tales."

"I have heard of these being in tales, but I had never thought of them to be real Father."

"There is another level where I have small creatures that are known to you as Fairies. Fairies are my favorite creatures, because they are small and beautiful. They have small wings but they are not used for flying. They wear their wings to be identified with the colors of their chosen flowers. They are the beautiful little creatures that go from place to place in order to spread greatness and beauty among all of our creations."

"What do they do?"

"They pass through many layers in order to achieve a lot. Their main task is to befriend the flowers and make sure they are well. They assist the flowers and our Gardens in order for them to look as beautiful as they can. They possess the ability to seek the wisdom of our side and translate this to the Gardens."

"Do Fairies work in the Gardens on our side or on the other side?"

"They work in Gardens on our side but they exist in the Underworld."

"Why do they exist in the Underworld, if they work in the Gardens on your side?"

"They chose to be in the Underworld because they wanted to be with the smaller creatures of their own habitat. They are magnificent small creatures but their lives are short and they don't live very long."

"Why is that?"

"They chose to live short so they can also evolve like you, but even more than you."

"I see"

"There is another level in the Underworld that is for larger creatures. What you describe as Dragon type creatures and their sole purpose is to protect your earth in order to save its' energy. They make sounds and noises that ward off evil presences by scaring them."

"What evil presences are you talking about?"

"There are energy forces that are not always good. These larger creatures are the protectors of the Underworld. They are never a threat to your being and existence as they serve me only, by protecting the Earth and all its' levels."

"I see"

****

"I like to conclude by saying that the Underworld is a place of Mystical creatures that you may have read about on your side. There are also other creatures that are not familiar to you and they all serve a purpose to our being. They were all created in order to serve; therefore, their small spirits are positive energies and elements. Although you don't directly feel and sense their existence you are to know and appreciate the work they do on behalf of our Earth.

"Thank you"

Lesson Seven – The Earth

"I have chosen to speak about the Underworld to you because the Underworld also depends on the level of care that is given and shown to our Earth. The Earth is a very important topic for us here. My people need to care better for Earth and the Universe they live in. You are to open my children's eyes in order to relay this message of caution to them."

"Yes, I will do my best."

"Your existence solely depends on the environment that you can live in. If they don't care for the environment, their being is in danger. You are here to learn but you must take care of this beautiful earth that is here for you. Your Ancestors took better care of this place than you have. Your needs have become so much that you are not seeing what you are doing. This is the time to be more cautious, because your existence as well as the existence of your future depends on your earth."

"I understand."

"There will come a time when you will be awakened to the damages that you have caused to this planet. Then you will try to fix those problems, however, it may then be too *late because you will have managed to destroy many levels of creation and existence among yourselves."*

"Yes, I hear you Father."

"Please keep in mind that our Earth is our Home and that we all need to make the effort to take care and love it from our hearts, minds and Spirits. I cannot say enough on this topic but I have said all I need to say on it."

****

"Let all live in Peace. However, keep in mind that Peace will only be there, if there is contentment among all creations. There has to be a balance between what you want and what you need."

Lesson Eight – The Council

"My Council is a group, which is composed of Elderly Spirits. They meet regularly and they are the beings who are responsible to letting me know of the conditions of our world, including of your level. They operate in the same manner as your large companies do there. They are my advisors and their responsibilities are to advise me about issues that relate to your world and about my children. They are like Supreme Rulers, but they work under me. Their advice is always sound and without any mistakes."

"Where do they meet?"

"They meet in a building that is specially designed for them and they welcome all Guides and Spirits who would like to meet with them. They listen well to what is relayed to them and they make important decisions on your behalves. Their views are all very different but they are able to operate within the same frame of mind. They are different as individuals but they think alike, because they are Great Spirits and they make great decisions for all of you."

"Who are they personally or individually Father?"

"*Their names were given to them during their past lives on Earth. Their names are not important to our conversation, but please know that they were great people in their lives and continue to be great Spirits on this side of our existence also.*"

"I see,"

"*The Council serves me and our needs here. They were given the ability to make sound decisions on your behalves, about your lives, homes, beliefs, experiences and things to come.*"

"Who are the Spirits that can approach the Council?"

"*The Council is usually approached by your Spirit Guides on your behalf when they need something for you from us. They know the rules and they are aware of our principles. The Council will meet with them and allow the Spirit Guides to make their cases as to what they need. When they agree to change something in your life's purpose, than they allow this information to be given to your Spirit and it will override any other information within your Spirit. They are capable of tapping into a level of your Spirit and describe these changes to your form, body and mind and they take effect.*"

"This process reminds me of our Court Systems here."

"*Yes, it is from the same principles where your Court systems were received from.*"

"Can an Individual Spirit meet with the Council?"

"Yes, they can but this is kept to minimal levels, because there is so much to do with your Guides and other great Spirits. This leaves a very small amount of time for individual Spirits. However, their concerns are relayed to the Council by the Master Teachers who are always with our other Spirits here."

"When a Spirit desires to come back to live on Earth, do they have to get permission from the Council or from you Father?"

"When a Spirit is ready and would like to reincarnate, they are given the abilities to do this their own selves. But, we do assist them in certain things. They are given our energies and plans to live by."

"What do you mean by plans?"

"They live according to a chart that they make themselves and they live accordingly to their plan in this chart."

"Do most people live according to their charts they made?"

"Yes, they do. However, there are people who change their minds once they are in Human Form on Earth. But, the plans that you made here are sounder for your own personal growth. Therefore, we encourage your Spirits to stay on their chosen plans when they are there."

"What happens if they don't?"

"This is their decision. They are free to make their own choices, but they may not always achieve what they have come there for."

"Why do Spirits come down here?"

"You are all produced from my great energy and it is your Spirit's longing desire to be perfect and to be with my greater energy. But, your Spirit needs to become great by evolving in order to be in form with mine. Your Spirit was from here and it would like to return home."

"Thank you for explaining this to me."

****

"To conclude our lesson, allow me to say that the Council of Elders is here to serve me but they also serve your needs there. Their tasks are very hard and they do their job with no mistakes. You are to be aware of their presence because when you need your Spirit Guide to come to them, they will know of you. They will care for you just as I do. They are here to be of accompany to your Spirit and you must know and appreciate this wisdom and guidance."

"Thank you."

"Now, you go in Peace and may Peace and good things always come to you."

Lesson Nine – My Children

"*I want to remind you of your purpose. You chose to live once again to have numerous opportunities to learn from and experience events that will further your spiritual growth. Your lives were given to you as a gift and it is to be treated as a gift, no matter who you are and what you have.*"

Yes"

"*I created people a very long time ago. But, when I created them, they were very simple and humble. They have prospered among themselves and they have become great beings. Their lives were not measured by whom they were. Their lives were measured by what they had done.*"

"What do you mean by saying what they had done?"

"*The tasks they completed, especially the tasks that served not only the person's own self but also the needs of other people. They have managed to help each other in many ways, but they have also managed to build blocks to their and each other's existence.*"

"Yes"

"You have chosen your lives in order to work on lessons of your own choice according to what you needed. Many of you will let go of your true desires that are given and seek elements that are less important for the greater being of your lives. Your accomplishments will distinguish your Spirit form those of others."

"What do you mean or in what way?"

"They will speak for themselves and they will present themselves to you personally."

"Who are you talking about when you say "they"?"

"Those people, whom you helped, people whom you fed, people whom you loved and those people who loved you. They will all be here to remind you of these accomplishments and then you will remember all things in its right and deserving way. When I selected the lives of the people whom I put on earth, I made sure that they were worthy and great Spirits to accomplish many things."

"Yes Father,"

"There are children in this world who are not cared for, but you neglect to see them. Their tears have dried out and their bodies are weak, but you choose not to see them. Many of your eyes don't see any more. They are blinded by your lack of concern for others."

"I understand"

"There will come a day when you will return home and find that you have not brought back anything with you that you accumulated in your lives. But what you will bring back

is your lessons of knowledge that you have gained from your existence on Earth."

"Yes"

"Then you will have the time to sit and review your lives and look at all the things that you have accomplished on earth in order to better yourself and the life of others. There will be many of you who will claim to have accomplished a lot, but your accomplishments must not just be visible to the eye."

"What do you mean Father?"

"I mean that your accomplishments should serve a great purpose for you and to others. Love each other with your Spirits, hearts and minds. Let all flourish equally among yourselves. There are plenty of all things and all of my children should be well cared for on this Earth. Let no man tell you that there is not enough. I have made sure that there are enough of all things necessary to exist with for all my children. You are to treat yourselves and each other with respect, love and understanding. There will come a day when all these will be shown to you by us."

"Yes"

"I allow no one to kill my children. I don't approve of people who are starving my children in order to make statements on my behalf. They know who they are and they will answer to me when they come home to our side. You are to not fear me, but you are to fear me if you are causing a great deal of unnecessary sadness and suffering to the children

of my world. I am very adamant about what I have said to you in this matter."

"I hear and understand you Father."

"There will be people who disregard what is being said but it is all well by me. They will know my words when I am to speak with them. They will acknowledge and admit to their wrongdoings on behalf of the children whom they harmed by starvation, lack of medicine, lack of compassion and lack of love. I am the last word; I am the last word for them. I will not tolerate these kinds of injustices. There will come a time when they will have to explain themselves to me and they will than present their reasons for the behaviors that I am witnessing."

"Yes"

"I love all my children and you are to let them know of this. There is no other God but me and that I make their world easier if I choose to. Those who choose to not learn will not grow within the levels they are functioning at. Those who learn will grow and evolve into the great Spirits that you are to become. There is plenty of time to correct your ways if you are on a wrong path. Your path should be clear, positive and full of valuable accomplishments not only for you but for others and for our Earth."

"Yes, I understand."

"I have brought many reminders to your earth but people don't see these gentle reminders that are occurring. They blame it on the environment, weather, sickness and other reasons that are acceptable to their minds. There are

greater reasons for my gentle reminders on Earth. You are to be aware of your own selves and see what is important and what is not."

"What are the important things Father?"

"The important things are very obvious but you neglect to see them. They are all about people. They are about people, of people and for people. They are the welfare of my children and you are to know what is important and what is not."

"Of course"

"You are to awaken and look around you, and open your eyes. Open your eyes so wide that you will be able to see everything. When you see everything, you will cry. You will see the grief of what is caused around the world, you will see things that scare you and you will see things that you have ignored all these years. This is the time of greater awakening. Because our lives have changed and we need to be greater now, than how we are."

"Yes"

******

"You are to remind my children that I am with them and that I see their misery around the world. I am among them. My love for you is endless. I will love those who serve me not only here but also there."

Lesson Ten – The Harm

"There are numerous lessons to learn from the disasters that are occurring on your Earth. These reasons are caused primarily by the people of the Earth. And there are more to come because people are not changing the way they live."

"What do you mean Father?"

"There have been changes within the atmosphere of the Earth. This is mainly due to the output of your chemicals that are within your atmosphere. These chemicals are dangerous and a source of the destruction that is being caused to your atmosphere. The people of the Earth will awaken, but I am afraid that their awakening may come too late for some of the harm that they have caused to their environments."

"Yes"

"These causes are due to many elements that are being used in order to live on Earth. There are many reasons but the primary reason being the use of chemicals that are produced from Petroleum products. These are harming your air and waters around the world. Their use and neglect is the primary cause of this destruction."

"What do you mean by destruction?"

"There are levels of atmosphere. The atmosphere level that is closest to Earth is being changed. Due to the fumes produced by your companies, vehicles, and like sources."

"Father, please excuse me but I am not a Scientist so can you please explain to me how this level is effected, so I can understand?"

"These elements that are found in the gases that are produced are lowering down the chemical makeup of your atmosphere and for this reason this layer is being harmed. Your reasons for the use of these chemicals are to survive but you don't need these chemicals in order to survive and to live on Earth. There are many other resources that you can substitute in order to not harm your Atmospheric level of needed gases."

"Yes"

"There is to be more harm done if the uses of harmful chemicals are to integrate into your air and then it will be very difficult to fix the caused problems from these. There needs to be public education and alert given to people and how they are causing this harm to the atmosphere. There are people in your world who are intelligent enough to find alternative ways of producing chemicals that are less harmful to your existence on Earth. But these people and their intelligence are not utilized in order to make more money. Their lives were specially planned so they are brilliant with the topics of the greater causes to preventing damages that are being done. Their names are clear to your leaders, but these issues and people are avoided as a topic."

"I see"

"Your world will not be the same as you know if you don't take measures to correct how you live and affect the world around you. I have given clear and gentle messages to my people on Earth; however these messages are being interpreted as caused by weather and other matter that is acceptable to one's conscious."

"What do you mean by gentle reminders?"

"I have caused some small and minor disasters in order to awaken people's thoughts and to make them think better but they are being disregarded by your people."

"Why are they being disregarded Father?"

"Your leaders are too busy looking at small topics to satisfy your small needs. They need to think better and bigger in order for your lives to improve and to remain at the levels that it is at. When you walk you have to look ahead of you, not just in front of your feet."

"Yes, I understand. I am also sorry."

"Your Ancestors lived much more simply. They had not discovered ways of living the way you have. However, their lives did not harm the world and you are destroying what they did not. Their lives may have been simpler but they were considerate of the world and its components. There were many times they also wanted great things to live with but they knew better at that time. Their needs were not as great as what yours have become."

"Yes"

"Your needs are to be measured by what you need to survive with, not by what you want. There is no one to impress but your own selves and right now you can't even impress your own selves. Because, your hearts have darkened and became selfish."

"I am listening"

"Your Sea Life has been affected by these selfish acts on your behalf. The creatures of the Sea have been suffering much and they are in the process of adjusting to their new lives and habitats in order to survive. Their needs are not being met and they are not well. They used to be a great component of your lives but now their lives are left for them to defend. They need for you to better keep and care for their environments. Your love for them is not enough. Your love for them should encompass preserving their homes and environments. Their lives depend on you and what you do to your Earth."

"I am listening Father,"

"Their existence has become more difficult and they are adapting and adjusting to new places and behaviors. Your needs will be met if their needs are being met and our needs don't come before theirs. I allow all things to survive in their natural environments and yours is not any more important than theirs. Their needs are equally important as yours and if they are not well cared for by you, they will not exist any longer."

"I don't know what to say. But, I am hearing your words."

"There is much time for many things but some things are at a greater importance and you are to make this the greatest importance to your lives. Your lives depend on these animals and creatures you are surrounded by. They have brought love and nurture to your lives and you are to respect and love them in return for their sacrifices they have to make. Please, awaken to your environmental destructions that you are causing to this Earth and love your home. Then you will learn to love your own selves more."

"Yes. I am lost in my words, but I am listening."

"Let there be peace among all my people, animals and creatures. Let people live peacefully and in harmony with their surroundings and each other."

"Thank you Father, anything else?"

****

"I made my point clear for you and you are to let my messages to spread to my people. Let them love all my creations not those whom they select."

Lesson Eleven – Afterlife

"What do you mean by Afterlife Father?"

"By After life I mean what happens to your Spirit once it departs from your level of being."

"I see"

"You are to remember that you are there temporarily and that your lives are measured by your achievement not by the length of time that you lived there. Your life purpose is to experience and to do great things for your selves. There are many opportunities for you to learn from while you are there. There will be times when life will get difficult because these are the moments that will build your character and life lessons for you."

"Yes, I understand."

"Your Afterlife consists of many steps and you are to know of these steps because you will all experience these events as you unfold from your bodies and lives that you are living in."

"What are these steps you are talking about?"

"When your body is ready to shut down your Spirit will take over. You will be confused at this time but not scared. Your Spirit will lead you to our Home here. Your bodies will age, become ill and there will come a day when you will make this transition to our side of life. Then you will be given opportunities to make more decisions for yourselves."

"Yes, I am listening to you Father."

"When I say Afterlife, I am talking about the life that continues after you depart from your existence on Earth. You will all make this journey. You don't need to fear it and you don't need to dwell on it either. There will be people here to help you and to accommodate you when you come here."

"Who are those people that you are talking about Father?"

"These will be people of your past and Spirit Guides who will greet and welcome you back. Then you will be made comfortable in order to rest your Spirit from your experiences that you have lived through on Earth. You will have a period of time to rest and be yourself once again."

"What do you mean by be yourself?"

"You will be given an amount of time to be well and whole again."

"What do you mean by whole?"

"Your bodies and minds will adjust back to its Spirit Form. You will leave behind your ailments, sickness' and worries. You will than feel well and whole again. Your bodies suffer while you live on Earth and this suffering also leaves

some memories to your Spirits. But your Spirit will heal and once again you will feel well in your newly discovered selves."

"I see, what happens after we are greeted by our loved ones and Spirit Guides and this transition time?"

"You will be adjusting to your life here and during this time you will have the opportunities to let go of all the past memories of your recent lives. Your minds will clear and your bodies will feel whole again."

"And then what Father?"

"Then you will make decisions for your own self. You will be introduced to larger and greater Spirits who will help you make better decisions."

"Better decisions for what?"

"To continue with another life or to stay here and rest awhile. These are your choices and you will have to make them yourself."

"If a Spirit would like to continue to live again, what happens?"

"Then that Spirit is given courses in order to prepare them for their new life on Earth."

"What do you mean?"

"There are ways to prepare Spirits for their new lives. This includes of educating them about their chosen places and lives they will be entering into."

"How long does that take?"

"This is a short period of time. If a Spirit would like to return to Earth than this must occur within a short period of time so that their Spirit does not adjust to the comforts of our side once again. This will be given to them by our Master Teachers in a prompt and a proper way. They will require you to make your own choices but advise you to make clear decisions."

"And if a Spirit chooses to not return to live right away, than what happens?"

"They are given chores here. They also have to work here and keep their selves busy with learned lessons and lessons we provide here."

"What kind of chores or work do the Spirits do on your side?"

"They can do many things, just like on Earth. But you will have the opportunity to use your entire self and accomplish much more."

"Is it the Spirit's choice to do what they would like to do?"

"Yes, it is their choice. But we also reflect on their strengths and utilize them in accordance with what they would like to do here."

"I see. Father, if I may backtrack to an earlier time, can you tell me about the initial moments when a person departs from here."

"Yes, of course. Their first experience will be to see a very bright light in order for them to know of their path. They will have the choice to go to this light form and then they will find our beings there waiting for them. They are welcomed by all people gathered there."

"I see. What else is there that you would like for us to know about afterlife Father?"

"You are not to fear dying, because dying is another part of your living. Death is a beginning of your life once again. There is to be no fear of death."

"Many people are afraid of death father."

"Yes, they are, because they have learned to fear death from others and they need to have no fear of death. There will be times when people are not ready to let go of their physical lives on Earth, but when they become aware of this side, they will feel comfortable to let go and let be."

"I am listening to you Father."

"You are to let my people know that they are not to fear death, it is another aspect of your living."

"I understand. Thank you."

"There are stages of Afterlife. During these stages you are given many things that will be helpful to you. During the first stage, you will be shown and have the opportunity to watch pictures of your life that you lived while you were in your human form. After you view these pictures, you will make sense out of what you lived through and how you dealt with things."

"And then,"

"Then you will be spoken to about your experiences and our teachers will give you feedback. Our Teachers will be with you during this process and explain to you what you did right and wrong in order to learn. They will review many things with you and their advice will be helpful to you in your growth."

"What happens after a Spirit reviews their life?"

"This is the final step to your being. You will be given the option to live again or be here longer in order to work through some of your issues that you may have not dealt with on the other side."

"I see"

"Yes, these are the steps to your Afterlife and they will be helpful to you and to your adjustment process."

"Father, here on Earth we are told about Heaven and Hell. Can you talk to me about this?"

"Yes. There is Heaven and that is our side. This is the Heaven they talk about because it's a peaceful place where there is only peace, and love always follows peace. There is no cruelty and other negative human emotions. It is a place of peaceful existence for all Spirits."

"Father as much as I don't want to talk about it, but you must know that people also want to know about what is Hell?"

"Yes, I know. This is also here. The word Hell comes from this side, but it is not as bad as how people portray it on your side. It is only a place where you will be shown the wrong things you have done on Earth and then you will be made to work on yourself."

"How do people work on their selves there?"

"You will be taught by great Spirits there, who are used to dealing with people like this. They will teach and show you lessons, through the goodness of their own Spirits. Their efforts are to teach you greater levels of functioning."

"I see. During an earlier lesson, we had spoken briefly about when a person kills another person. Is this where they go?"

"No, this is not where they go. They go to a completely different location than here. Their Spirits are not within my World here. They are with another creator that they chose to follow and he will deal with their Spirits."

"Father, who is this other creator you speak of?"

"Yes, you are to know of him but not to fear him because he is a dark spirit and he is to lead those Spirits who are making great tragedies of killing other Spirits on Earth."

"So, you have no contact with him?"

"No, I don't. I don't care to either. He functions on his own and for this reason he is a dark spirit."

"How did he come about Father?"

"He was created from those Spirits who were very dark and his great energy is very grim. But today he has become a great energy of his own self and he operates under this image."

"Father, is there anything else to say about him?"

"Yes, you are not to think of him or talk about him because he is not a great being. His presence is not worthy of your white spirit. You will have no reason to talk about him or to be with him as long as you are being the best person you can be on Earth. There will be no further time given to his presence, because he doesn't deserve the greater senses of our own selves."

"I see. Thank you. Can we talk further about Afterlife?"

"The Children of God will once again reunite here and then you will see among yourselves those people that you met and loved. You are to be proud of your lives; they are difficult and hard there. When you arrive here, we will take very good care of you and nourish your Spirits once again."

"Thank you. Would you like to say anything else about Afterlife Father?"

"Yes. Please let all my people know that the Afterlife they imagine is to be of love and comfort to them. They are to have no fear of anything on this side because you are the Master of your own existence and lives. You are to love your own selves and those who surround you. Let their lessons be your lessons of learning. Live well and love each other as though this is your last breath. There is no promise of tomorrow to anyone

and you are to think that this is your last breath and live accordingly to your senses that I have given you."

"Yes"

"You now be in peace my child and let people know that you are well and let them know that you are hearing my words of comfort to yourselves. You are to be in peace always and may good things always come to you."

"Thank you"

Lesson Twelve – The Other Side

"You wanted a tour of this side. Today, I will tell you about some of our buildings and other places that exist on this side."

"Yes, thank you and I am listening to you."

"The Other Side is a term we use only to relate this side of our being and place to you. But, I don't like the word "Other Side", because it sounds very simple and common. This place is not simple as you may imagine and it is not for common people either. Therefore, you are not to imagine this place in your human minds as a place like there. But, think of it as a greater place than what you have seen there and much more greatness is put into it than your level of existence."

"I apologize for using the term Other Side also, as there is no other way to describe it to others."

"I know what you are meaning. I understand your expressions you use in order to relate these words to people there."

"Thank you."

"I like to tell you that this side, our place here, was designed very carefully so it accommodates all of us who we need here. Therefore, of course there are buildings and great places that are here, but most important is being that our Spirits have a peaceful place of their own. There are beautiful buildings and structures here but there are places that need to be further created also. There is plenty of time to make many more things and we have great Spirits who are capable of doing things and working hard to make them possible. They make this place beautiful, more beautiful than how you can imagine it to be."

"I can only imagine Father, and that is probably not enough."

"We have specially designed prominent buildings for different purposes but also smaller places to accommodate our small needs. The larger buildings are those to accommodate our Great Spirits here."

"What buildings are those Father?"

"The most important building is our Council's building. This is like your Congress there. Our Elderly Spirit Council members exist and live here. This building is specially designed and made for their comforts. They serve a very important role in our lives therefore they deserve to be in a building that is as great as they are.

"How was this building made and what is it made from?"

"The buildings we have are made perfect and entirely from the minds' of our Spirits, who have remarkable

Engineering skills. They create and build places so grand and large that you would have a difficult time understanding. They use materials that are not found on your side, because they are specially equipped with elements that allow their presence to be magnificent. They are built with the minds but they exist within real physical senses."

"I see. Are there other buildings?"

"Yes, there are many other buildings, but for the purpose of this lesson we will discuss some important ones for you to know."

"Thank you"

"We have many other halls that are specially designed to house our teachers and other great Spirits. They reside within the boundaries of these places. They were also built with great care and love for them. Their buildings are slightly more different in that they are not as big as our Council's. However, much larger and impressive than any structure you have there. They are well kept and preserved for our use of them."

"What other buildings or structures are there father?"

"There are also large spaces to accommodate our host Spirits who are here with us. Their homes are within these spaces and they are also beautiful. They are built by Master builders who took great care and honor building them for their fellow Spirits."

"Can you tell me a little more about the structure of them?"

"*They look like glass but they are not exactly glass. They are visible to our Spirits but not to your eyes.*"

"What do you mean?"

"*They are magnificent buildings that are built by different forms of construction. They are built by minds not hands as you may imagine. They are very cleverly built by the highest forms of our builders and their great minds.*"

"I see"

"*There are many places. Some of them are for education and some are there for entertainment. They all serve a purpose and are to be used appropriately for what they are designed for. Our buildings are specially designed for our Spirits, for this reason they are given special abilities to serve our needs.*"

"What do you mean by that?"

"*They are created so they please our selves here. They house us but they also produce certain energies which replenish our Spirits with elements that we seek in order to be greater in our forms. They serve us and we serve them.*"

"I am listening"

"*You are wondering what else is there?*"

"Yes Father, I was."

"*There are beautiful gardens here to serve our needs to be in nature as we deserve to be in. Our Gardens are beautiful and offer the blooms of much different type of flowers, of some which you have there and many more."*

"Who are the Gardens kept by?"

"The Gardens are kept by the Spirits here but they are also given assistance from our Underworld Creatures. Our Gardens are always in beautiful form and bring much happiness to our being. We also have waters here and we use them for reflection. We reflect our selves and we swim. Your dense bodies stay below waters, but our Spirit remains on top of the waters where we can reflect and enjoy its presence."

"Do Spirits also enjoy waters like we do?"

"Yes, we also have fun like you do but in a different form than you. The waters also bring great joy and happiness to our being here. We are capable of swimming like you but within the limits of our own forms and minds. We enjoy the waters like you but just in a different manner."

"I see."

"There are many places, but the important ones are the ones I have talked to you about. You are to let people know that our lives here are like yours, but at a very high and intelligent way of living. On this side, your Spirit is able to take you anywhere you desire. Your mind is used One Hundred Percent and you will be able to do many things with it."

"Anything else you would like to say about the Other Side, Father?"

"Yes, the Other Side is a place of Peace and Beauty. Let all know that this is our entire home. We exist peacefully among our own selves and we make all feel included in our home. You are to live under the same principles on Earth because there will come a day when you will have to live like this here. You are to be kind and treat each other with respect, in order to feel each other's presence. Then you will be able to see and appreciate each other's selves and Spirits."

"Yes Father,"

"When you arrive here, you will see this magnificent place yourselves and then you will remember. You will than know where you are and how you came here. We welcome you always and you are always welcomed to your home."

"Thank you Father."

Conclusion from the Author

I was very honored and humbled by the words of the Beloved Father God within these lessons he offered me. I share them with the readers as it was his wishes for them to be shared. Although our lessons were on twelve topics I realize that life is full of lessons and that there is a deeper purpose for all things on this Earth. I wish for these lessons to bring peace, love and a greater understanding into our lives and minds.

These Lessons with Father God were also a great learning opportunity for me and I became aware of greater issues and of my own self during my meditations with him. I realize there is so much more to learn from and within our lives on this Earth. Although, reading about the spiritual experiences of other people has paved a walkway for my spirit, we are to find, seek, and search our own spiritual paths.

Father God's presence is always calm and peaceful. He explains all things in a gentle but a cautious way. These lessons were given to me with love and I pass them to you with love. Blessed be.

Conclusion from my Spirit Guide, Manalan

"There are many lessons in life, but some carry a greater importance to your being. Those are the love for your selves and to others. They enfold all we need to know and to be like, because this is our way of being here. Your human bodies were meant to live a short life and to learn as much as you can in your chosen lives and those lessons you learn will play a great importance to your Spirits. There is no time but now, and this time does not exist but within your minds. Time is essential on your side but there is no time on our side. We look at person's level of being, not how long they have lived. The purpose of your lives is to live. Live to learn, learn to believe, believe to know and when you know, your mind and body will find peace and comfort."

Conclusion from the Beloved

"My Children, I have spoken and I have spoken through this woman to you. I speak through many of your people there and sometimes they are afraid to say that they speak with me. Their words come through their hands but those words start with my Spirit and they make it possible to let you know of our thoughts and wishes. You are not to doubt anything but your own selves. When you doubt the words of another you are closing your minds to further learning and discovery. You don't need to fully understand or accept all you hear but keep your minds open to our messages. Our messages are of joy, love, compassion and concern. Let there be peace on Earth, let there be peace among all children of this Earth, let there be peace among all animals and creatures of this Earth and you are to start this peace within your own minds."